BEING

a Memoir

M000312813

SHAKIA *Artson*

BEING

Being

A Memoir of Truths, Lies, & Intentional
Mishappens...

Shakia Artson

KICKIN IT

KICKIN IT
Kickin it Productions LLC
https://www.kickinitwithkia.com

Copyright © 2021 by Shakia Artson
All rights reserved. No part of this publication may be reproduced, distributed, or transmitted in any form or by any means, including photocopying, recording, or other electronic or mechanical methods, without the prior written permission of the publisher, except in the case of brief quotations embodied in critical reviews and certain other noncommercial uses permitted by copyright law. For permission requests, email the publisher with subject title: "Copyright Request" at the email address below.

Library of Congress Cataloging-in-Publication Data
Names: Artson, Shakia, author.
Title: A Memoir, Being / Shakia Artson
ISBN: 978-1-7368964-1-9 (Paperback)
ISBN: 978-1-7368964-0-2 (Digital Online)
Library of Congress Control Number: 2021907729
Subjects: Poetry, Memoir
First Edition: August 2021

Printed by IngramSpark, a division of Lightning Source LLC, in the United States of America.

Cover image: *Blossom into your Being*
Photography by Frank Pimentel
Cover design by Iris Designs
Book design by Shakia Artson

Any references or resemblence to historical events, real people, or real places are used fictitiously or entirely coincidental. Names, characters, and places are products of the author's imagination.

contact@kickinitwithkia.com

To brown girls on city streets, never forget where the light lives...

Always remember bus stops & train rides.

FOREWARD

By: Ronide Comeau
@anxiousblackgirlcomics, 14.6K

From being high school classmates, running in student government together, and now witnessing Shakia grow into the phenomenal woman she is today, it truly is an honor to write about the significance of her life and story, "Being."

Shakia takes us on a heartfelt journey, capturing the true essence of what it's like to be a black girl growing up in Brooklyn. With each milestone, a lesson is formed to remind us that even through the midst of darkness, there is always a tunnel leading to the light. To the black girls who feel alone, misunderstood, and trapped - this book is for you.

Not only will her words remind us of the power, which lies in vulnerability; they showcase the black voice in a society where there is a lack of black representation. Hear me clear: seeing a black woman heal and thrive is not only inspiring, it is imperative.

In the words of Maya Angelou, "The greatest gift we give to each other is the telling of the truth." I personally do not know what's more powerful than that.

Thank you Shakia; for your wisdom, strength, transparency, and most importantly [thank you] for being you.

Black girls need more role models and I'm thrilled to know that they now have you.

CONTENTS

PART ONE: BEING BORN

01

Being Light

As I sit in Accounting class, with my head down and headphones blasting, I hear a huge BANG in the hallway—who's fighting today? I immediately get up from my seat and rush into the hall only to find an agitated teacher in a hopeless attempt to calm down a crying and irritated student. I peak into his classroom, to see her remaining peers in a state of laughter. Now, gliding over to the hysterical girl and gently pushing the teacher out the way, I escort her into the adjacent stairwell—we aren't best of friends, but she trusts me more than the dominant figure who previously stood before her. She crumbled in full surrender to me—a young girl crying, shaking, and ready to kill the world—as I long to offer her some stability amidst her insecurity.

After a moment of tugging and pulling, I am finally able to calm her nerves. By this time, one of my principals is standing in the doorway onlooking the situation. I rush past her, march right through the teacher, and storm into his classroom. I begin to express my disappointment in and disgust with all the seated young girls' behavior. Regardless of the situation, there is always a less demeaning way to get a point across. Now, the classroom is full of silence. I am unaware if any of my words will fall on solid ground, but it at least makes them all ponder for a moment. I vaguely remember the details of the altercation, but I know when I took that young girl into the stairwell, she looked at me for help—there was a fear in her eyes that reached far beyond the girls in her classroom. Later that year, the same young girl was slaughtered and killed by her mother's boyfriend, who had been sexually abusing her for years.

McAuley was about a 200 person (faculty and staff included) catholic high school in the East Flatbush area of Brooklyn, NY. My mother saw fit to enroll me in an all girls' institution, due to my previous actions – but we'll get into that later.

<blockquote>
I may not be able to rescue them from their abusive step-father or lingering low self-esteem, but I can be a light.
</blockquote>

During my senior year, McAuley went through an intense transitional period. A portion of our already small faculty retired, which caused positions to shift abruptly. The moving of our Dean of Discipline to a Librarian position was one of those big shifts that affected everyone. This stint meant our principals would enforce disciplinary action with the help of the elected student government.
And you guessed it—not only was I on student government, but I was student body co-president.

Overall, I was a decent student with a heart to help people, but Lord knows I didn't want to be a role model, because that's terrifying.

But, my titles as president, editor of the newspaper, peer mediator, and counselor, put me in a position that would change my life forever. I went into senior year already having developed a relationship with the girls at my school.

They weren't just any girls—they were my girls. I knew some more intimately than others, but nonetheless, I still loved and cared for all of them. There was a light in me that would have never been able to shine at its fullest potential; if not, for the standard they held me to.

As my best friend and I walk into school late into 2nd period, Ms. Laconte, school secretary, stops us.

"School started almost 2 hours ago, Ms. Artson."

Chantelle swoops in to rescue me, "The 46 was messed up this morning—you know snow and stuff." By now, Ms. Lake, one of our principals, is outside of her office.

"Well you two need to hurry up, change into your uniforms, and go to class. Shakia, you know better." Chantelle and I drag our feet towards the hall. Every time we walk past a classroom, I feel as if all the students and teachers are staring at me.

I lean over to Chantelle, "Yo, I don't know why people think I'm perfect—like, it's f*cking snowing outside—you thought I was going to ride a plow to school this am?"

Chantelle, always playing devil's advocate, "I mean, you was just going in on someone yesterday for always being late." I roll my eyes. As I begin to open my locker, I debate on whether or not I should put my entire uniform on—I feel like being lazy. Then, one of my girls walks up to me and points to her feet, "See, I got my shoes on today just for you." I force a smile and say to myself, "Guess I better get to changing…"

This is just one of the many examples of how my girls constantly forced me to be better. Even times when I felt like slacking, cutting class, wearing an incomplete uniform, or bashing someone's head into a wall—knowing they were watching me, kept me in check. Not to say I was a perfect student, because everyone knew I broke the rules at times. I believe my short-comings made me more relatable, which encouraged others to follow my lead even more. I'm convinced God put all those people in my life to serve as the key to unlock the next level of my potential. Shondaland's *Scandal* character, Olivia Pope has taught me,

"The truth is like the sun; you can shut it out for a time, but it ain't going away."

Similarly, I believe we all have an immense amount of truth in us that longs to get out to the rest of the world. There is a constant battle within myself:

Either be a beacon of light to others or allow my light to be dimmed by life's hardships?

No, perfection is not an option; we all fail and fall short, but no mistake can ever make your light disappear. When my girls look to me for help, I may not be able to rescue them from their abusive step-father or lingering low self-esteem, but I can be a light. I can be a vessel, which brightens their dark paths, even if only for a brief moment. There was something everyone within those four walls saw in me that I could not see in myself. A luminous light, which had been planted in me from birth. I couldn't save all my girls from every gloomy Brooklyn Street, but they saved me from myself.

02

Being Brooklyn - *Child's Play*

"Okay Ma, I'm out!"
"Stay between the stop sign and that last house—right befo-
re the park."
"Come on Ma, can I please go to the park? All my friends
are there."
"No."
"But, Glen gets to go to the–"
"Glen is older—you're 10—and can always stay inside for
the rest of the summer."
"Can I at least take some of my dolls out?"
"SHAKIA GO! Better be in this house when them street
lights come on."

I bolt out of my mother's room and head straight for
the living room. I pick up two of my nicest dolls—both
brown skinned—one a doctor and the other an ice skater.
My mother never bought me white dolls.
There was always a speech in Toys R Us, about how when she
was coming up, *there weren't any black dolls.* So she would
only buy me, her only daughter, a brown or ethnic looking
doll as long as she lived.

With two dolls in hand, I open the front door, and
head outside. My grandmother is sitting on the stoop talking
to Ms. Marshall, Mr. Percy is across the street on his grill, and
an array of kids are running up and down the block playing
"Red Light, Green Light, 123." I say hello to Ms. Marshall
and my grandmother, as I walk a few houses down, where
Kayla, Asia, and Domo are sitting on Asia's stoop.
"Hey yall, what's up?" They look up at me in confu-
sion.

"Where you going with your dolls, girl?" says Domo.

"I thought we could play on the stoop like we did yesterday."

Asia interjects, "Oh na, we're out to the park."

Kayla attempts to comfort me, "We'll come back and play with you later." Then, they all agree in unison as they walk toward the park without me.

I smile and say, "It's cool—I'm straight."

I sit on the stoop alone and play with my dolls, until a young boy with an oversized t-shirt and basketball shorts comes and sits next to me. Decades later; every time I come back to Brooklyn, I [still] find myself on a cracked stoop, with that same boy [now grown man], regardless of weather or circumstance.

I grew up in a 3-story brownstone home, along a tree-lined block, in the middle of Bed-Stuy, Brooklyn. Where, as long as the sun was out, there was always a beat bumping, burger grilling, or child playing—everyone stayed on the block, because that's where connections were made. By one's teen years, the friends you made on the block became your family. Meaning, if Ms. Debbie saw you doing something out of order, she had the right to pop you in your mouth and then tell your grandmother, so you'd receive a double pop. We had disagreements and quarrels like siblings, but we looked out for each other.

One day, a boy who didn't usually hang out on my block, started to make fun of me in front of my brother's friends. Suddenly, a boy who was never that nice to me, arose in my defense, *"If you say one more thing I'm beatin' your ass!"* The unfamiliar boy assessed the situation, realized he was outnumbered, and quickly walked away. That day, I realized all the kids , who I grew up with in PS 262 Park—hung out on the stoop, and ate Mr. Softee ice cream beside—were my family. No matter our differences, we were down for each other.

One summer day, we're all sitting in the park playing dominoes, when one of the older guys on the block comes up to my brother and says,

"Take off your hat and them shades."

"What?" My poor brother is so confused.

OG reiterates, "This young cat over here wanna fight you, so y'all finna have a fair one right now."

My brother looks at his friends for confirmation and then back at the OG—he obliges. Before I know it, my brother is standing in the dirt fighting this boy, because of something extremely miniscule—actually, the fight was because of me. Oops.

Nonetheless, I was surprised with the way my brother handled himself. Glen has always been known as a lover and not a fighter, but that day he held his own. There were no guns or knives, and when the situation got too hectic, the OGs broke it up.

That day, everyone walked away with their heads high—whether in victory or defeat. To some, that may have just been a regular street fight, but it taught me to approach my problems head on and never live in fear of failure. Also, as elders in the situation, they were trying to teach us strength and courage. Till this day, I take that courage with me into every classroom, board meeting, or overall professional setting.

Well, we aren't young kids running after the ice cream truck on a cool summer evening anymore. We're all grown up now and are forced to live out the repercussions of our social standings within America.

Meaning, being black and from the inner city doesn't leave one with too many options—though my counterparts who believe in "individualism" would disagree. I remember, all of us growing up with the same sparkle in our eyes, and while some are doing well, most are in jail, dead, wrapped up in illegal activity, or just living out our addictions [day by day] with no real future goals or ambitions.

Brooklyn has taught me many things, but one of the most important lessons I've learned is:

The real war in our low-income neighborhoods are not on the actual streets; it is inside the minds of the children who occupy those streets. At a certain age, our minds involuntarily tell us we cannot achieve, which is reflected in our rebellious actions. Social reproduction causes people to start viewing work as a means to an end—something that has to be done so we can barely get by. Towards the end of high school, we all begin to realize what track life has put us on and by that time, very few of us possess the resources or social means needed to project ourselves onto a different track. Whether right or wrong, I'd give anything to go back to those days when everything was just child's play.

03

Being Intellect - *Out of the Box*

"I think it's appropriate to send her upstairs."
"Well, that's nice, but how'd you decide this?"
"Her test scores are off the charts...
and she always distracts the other students when she fini-
shes her work early…"
"Okay, if it don't work out, she can always just come
back?"
"Yea, she can always just come back."

It is the beginning of the 2nd school quarter, as Ms. Fowler escorts me upstairs to the 5th floor of St. John the Baptist Catholic School. I'm petrified because I've been with the same kids, through better or worse, since Kindergarten, and I know nothing about life beyond 6th grade. She hands me a few of my new textbooks and brings me to Ms. Claudia's classroom. As I stumble, she places a soft hand on my shoulder and reinforces,

"Don't worry, you'll be fine—just remember why you're here."

I walk in and am suddenly faced with *a different world*. The girls have perms and the guys look like they should be on the cover of "The Source" magazine. I'm exaggerating, but you get my point. Sensing my fear,

"Hi Doll, I'm Ms. Claudia, take a seat anywhere and do the activity on the board please."

I hold my books tight, as I slowly walk to the nearest open seat, but of course I'm met with opposition.

"Um, this my seat, Ms. Piggy."

It's my first day, so I shake it off and slide further back

to another open seat. I'm about to sit down until–

"Na, you can't sit here–"

"Watch me b*tch." I plop my behind in the wooden desk, open my books, and begin to do the activity.

An array of "Ohhhhhs" and "Ahhhhhhs" can be heard in the background, as the girl next to me looks over and says,

"Hi, I'm Mia, it seems like we have one thing in common."

"Oh yea, what's that?" She reaches out her hand,

"I'm allergic to bullsh*t too." She's the first friend I made upstairs and we stayed friends until the day we graduated from 8th grade.

St. Johns was the beginning of people trying to put me in a box. Oftentimes, peers ended up disappointed with the outcome of their assumptions about me. The kids upstairs expected me to be timid, afraid, and clueless because I was smart enough to skip a grade. False! I was loud, had a sailor's mouth, and still managed to stay on first honors every quarter. Then, when I got back on my block,

"Omg you're actually smart."

"Why would I be dumb?" Another homie chimes in,

"I don't know, you're just so–" I interject,

"Much like you."

Growing up, there was always a distinction between being urban and being intelligent. I confused people, because I embodied both naturally. A regular night in my household consisted of my grandmother watching "Murder She Wrote," while my father listened to Onyx, as my mother gave me and my brother spelling quizzes. There was always an array of educated people around me, who were genuinely a part of and engaged with black culture. Brooklyn culture. Street culture.

It's the beginning of freshman year of high school. We don't know each other too well, but we're way pass the puppy-eyes phase of friendship. During free period, there is a very heated discussion taking place at my table–

"I don't care, Lil Kim is still the queen."
In objection, "But, Nicki bodied that verse." Now agitated,
"Look, I love Nicki—she's killing things right now, but Kim is still the queen... that's what's wrong with this generation—always want to put people on a pedestal before they actually prove themselves." Another friend in amusement,
"This generation? HA! Okay, Lady of Rage." I can't help but laugh,
"Na, but let's be serious, Nicki's been on a few DVDs & released a mixtape, but at this point, it's disrespectful to even mention her in the same sentence as Kim, son."

Suddenly, the bell rings. As we slide out the cafeteria, the conversation moves into the hallway. A couple of us enter our English class chatting. Our english teacher, Ms. Phillipe quickly settles us, as we prepare for the habitual "Free Writing" session.
Our topic is love. Ms. Phillipe puts the timer on and we begin to write. Moments later, I volunteer to read an excerpt of my writing:

"I think it is impossible for love to be a definitive term, because it encompasses numerous definitions heavily based in one's culture and upbringing. In Death of a Salesman, we see how Willy thinks the ultimate act of love is sacrificing his own life, to force his son to fulfill the future he sees as the most successful—though against Biff's aspirations. Contrarily, in A Raisin in the Sun, due to Mama's love for her son, she eventually goes against her religious beliefs and gives him money to build a liquor store..."

The entire class stares blankly at me. They're in disbelief. Why is there only one dimension of intelligence or success? I have felt this tension my entire life. Even in college, students find it complimentary saying, *"Oh wow, I didn't think you would be this smart,"* or *"Dang, you work so hard."*

Yes, my parents have instilled an unmatched work ethic, yearn for education, and ability to turn up in me [in no particular order either].

Fortunately, I've been able to prosper despite these stereotypes, but many of my inner-city counterparts don't. They are plagued with the falsehood, which says, "If you're smart, then you must behave, dress, and speak like this." I miss all the people I grew up with. I wish they were with me in college, on a mission trip, or study abroad program—but they're not. Many of them took different routes and I don't judge them for it, because I know how hard it is to go against the grain. But if I could tell them one thing, it would be:

Continuously, define culture, by first thoroughly learning all the rules, so you can break them in the most educated way possible.

In hindsight, if you put me in a box, not only am I going to climb out, I'll construct a cardboard car [out of it] and drive away with Notorious BIG on blast. #PERIODPooh

04

Being Hip Hop - *Brown Sugar*

"When did you fall in love with Hip Hop?"
"When my father played KRS-One's 'Return of the Boom Bap'"
"What did that do to you?"
"It made me feel powerful."

It is the summer of 2002, I'm running around the house in a frenzy because my brothers won't let me play their Dreamcast. To them, it's socially unacceptable for a girl to possess a controller amongst a room of teen boys. Being the only girl has some downfalls—not really though, because I still get whatever I want [oops]. I run pass my grandma's room crying. Ignored. Pass mommy in the bathroom. Ignored. Upstairs to my aunt. Ignored.

As I'm about to lose my spoiled mind, daddy calls me into the living room. He's sitting like a giant, organizing his cassette tapes and CDs with an intentional look of authority on his face. I stand there, out of breath, red eyes, and puffy eyelids, as I await his sympathy. But, he doesn't wrap me in his arms and say,

"You're daddy's little princess—" at least not in the way I expect him to. Instead, he inserts a disc into his black box stereo, fiddles with the buttons, and turns the speakers up loud. He holds steady eye contact with me, as he mouths, "We will be here FOR-EVER..." The base and snares comfort me as KRS-One attacks my chest.

I drift away into another consciousness with a thumb in mouth, close eyes, and open ears. Casting dreams are no longer on my radar, because I just want more of the *Boom Bap.*

Honestly, I don't know how to talk about my love for Hip Hop, without sounding artistic and extremely unsubstantial. But, there is no authentic way for me to offer you a front row seat into my being, without expressing my adoration for this cultural phenomenon. The art form, that makes room for anger, urban ideology, and the oppressed black soul.

Hip Hop is one of the very few spaces black men can feel safe. Guaranteed, I am not a black man, but black men helped raise me and they sit in the center of my heart. This means, I embrace those things that serve as a guiding light for them in the midst of their darkness. The beat offers room for the insecure black man, who doesn't know real love or luxury. It creates a cloud atop of the world they've always dreamed for—one of freedom and importance.

Later, this same freedom was offered to the black woman—a platform where the female MC is able to release her

So, if I was Sydney, and you ask me, "When did you fall in love with Hip Hop?"

It would have to be when I realized how much power it gave me.

frustrations about and hopes for the world she lives in. She can take control of her black body and show the world, that oppression no longer resides in her psyche. We are able to use wordplay, slick metaphors and smooth similes, to defy America's subconscious. We are free to rewrite the narrative of the silenced black story. Given space to retell our brokenness through fluid testimonies and active external battles. I am proud of the powerful poetic movement, which is Hip Hop.

I'm 14 years old, with a big mouth and tender-head, so you can imagine the conniption I'm having as my cousin braids my hair. She takes her time, as she runs her fingers through my coarse fro. Trying her best to grab every strand, because tomorrow is class pictures and I have to look fly.

As she braids and I cry, Mary J Blige is playing in the background—we're bumping to Reflections: A Retrospective. There aren't many verbal exchanges, but my cousin and I are bonding. She, along with MJB, are teaching me about womanhood and how to handle myself in certain situations. They comfort me and let me know that I am neither the first or last female in the world with a broken heart. Then, Blige spits a line, which halts my cousin in her tracks. She stops everything, pauses the stereo, and gives me a 15-minute hood story lesson.

I nod in agreement, even though, at the time, I have no real knowledge of the dope boys, struggles, or unwritten street creed she speaks of—all I know is, that this is important. As my head throbs, I listen intently, because this retrospective will be one of the building blocks that gets me through Brooklyn streets and ultimately life.

Essentially, my future is a mere time capsule of my history. Hip Hop is one of the defining factors of that capsule. It encompasses all that I am—from slave to savior, villain to victim, and hurt to hero. My journey is told through DJ spins, beatbox analogies, and rhymes from the dopest MCs.

Whether, during the late 80s, in the South Bronx singing, "the bridge is over" or screaming, "fight the power" in LA with Public Enemy—this is my history. I'll never forget, when Tink's diary helped me survive the Coldest Winter Ever. When I'm bouncing down the Freeway with State Property jamming, catching Deja Vu with Twenty88, or shaking to a TDE or Quality Control beat with my home girls, before we turn the dial to a Ladies' Night anthem by the Queen, I'm living out my forefathers' antiquity. Even if Eve needs to remind me "Love Is Blind," while my inner dog barks to a "Ruff Ryders' Anthem, " I know that I am not alone.

Ranging from new to old school, conscious or turn up; I have respect for the culture that made me. Hip-hop is not just music; it is culture. This is living, breathing, and engaging culture. Which, gives power to the muffled voices inside our cities [the voices of poverty, hurt, inequality, and shame]. I hear my voice when I turn on Power105 or Hot97—there is a phenomenon filled with justified rage in these voices.

So, if I was Sydney, and you ask me, "When did you fall in love with Hip Hop?" It would have to be when I realized how much power it gave me.

05   Being Consistent -
 Ode to my Parentals

"I'll pay $500 cash for ya spot in line"
"Oh na playa—we can't give up this spot—our son's been
waiting on this WII"
"But, my wife told me, if I don't have this system—DON'T
COME HOME"
"Well, it's some cheap motels uptown bruh, but we've been
out here since 6am—and we're not moving...NOW STEP!"

The hour is 8am on a chilly day in NYC. It's the week
before Christmas and picture the scene: an action-packed
42nd street filled with frazzled parents. Endless amounts
of parental duos rushing around, attempting to get their ki-
ddies all the goodies—they may or may not deserve. My
parents have traveled on a packed A train from Brooklyn to
the legendary *Toys R' US Times Square* location in hopes to
secure a *WII* for my older brother Glen. As they stand on a
line, which wraps around 2 corners, a man approaches and
pleads,
    "Can I please have your space in line? I'll pay cash."
My father in disbelief,
    "Na playa—our son's been begging for this WII and

we gotta get it." Offering another attempt,

"Come on man, it's sold out everywhere and my wife told me, if I don't have this system—don't come home." My mother, now agitated,

"Listen—we've been out here since 6am and there were people already in line, who slept here all night—you can't have our spot—now STEP!"

Eventually, the man walks off; my parents get inside, get their hands on this high-demand WII, and secure another hood Christmas victory.

Here's the thing about my parental duo: they have always given me [extremely] more love than I can ever give back in return.

I cannot count the amount of dollars spent on Catholic school tuition, church recitals, field trips, old-fashioned cookies from Kings Plaza, or cheddar biscuits from Red Lobster at Gateway Mall.

"

Whether standing on a long-a** line for a game system or moving their lives across country so their only daughter can pursue her dreams—their sacrifices never go unnoticed. Growing up, I saw their ways as more of an annoyance, than a sacrifice.

But, as I reflect, there's literally nothing in this world, they would/will not do for me. I cannot count the amount of dollars spent on Catholic school tuition, church recitals, field trips, old-fashioned cookies from Kings Plaza, or cheddar biscuits from Red Lobster at Gateway Mall.

It is impossible to accurately record the times their sacrifices have made me smile, because I don't think there is a number big enough to capture all the instances their love has broken my fall.

Have we always gotten along? Of course not. In fact, I personally took my duties as the last child and only girl very seriously. Meaning, I had to be extra, spoiled, and sassy—how did my parents survive me? Also, I was quite an angry child and disturbed adolescent, but even my worst behavior couldn't shake them.

Shaking immensely, as my mother scolds me,

"See this is the sh*t I'm talking about—do you see what time it is Shakia?"

A glance at the microwave exposes greenish numbers, which showcase a late 11:12pm. With no response, my head hangs low, in hopes to victimize my way out of this. But, since this is the 4th time I've come home late for the month, my mom isn't down to play the victim game. Now even louder,

"Umm HELLO! You ain't got sh*t to say? Where you been? Coming in my house on a Wednesday this time of night... have you lost your f*cking mind?" In need of a quick excuse,

"Ma, I told you the newspaper prints tomorrow and I'm the editor ... like it ran late and the 46 was wildin'—I'm not even lying." [I was DEFINITELY LYING] My mom, not buying the lies I'm selling,

"Yea whatever. You think you're grown and that's the problem—I hope whoever you been with has a bed for you to sleep on when I put your a** out!" Now upset [because I definitely wasn't with a boy],

"Whatever! I don't want to talk about this anymore. I'm tired!" As I attempt to walk pass my mother, she grabs my hand tight with focused eyes fierce enough, to remind me who she is. She whispers,

"Please don't make me beat you down like a stranger on the street who stole my man."

She releases my scared body, I stomp upstairs, and SLAM! *Why did I just slam my door?* My brother Glen, peaks in and begins to shake his head in disbelief,

"I told you to stop talking back, but NOOOO. You always gotta get her like this..." My mom, now directly behind him,

"Great! You're awake—take this door off the hinges now." Glen takes a beat, in hopes she'll change her mind. But, Toni always means what she says and continues,

"I told you, keep slamming my damn doors and you won't have one."

Within the next hour, my door, phone, directv box, and computer keyboard/mouse [yup, my mom left the monitor] were all confiscated from my room for at least the next month. Toni was queen of the "spank and punish" club. During my younger years, punishment pierced harsher than my mother's belt. Friends constantly heard,

"Yea, Shakia's still on punishment. DON'T CALL MY HOUSE FOR 2 WEEKS!"

But, what did it teach me? For one, only a petty black woman would think to confiscate her child's keyboard/mouse while simultaneously leaving the desktop monitor situated perfectly in the same child's room. *Right?* But, in all seriousness, without my mom's wit and stern demeanor, I probably wouldn't have made it out of the jungle. Immense gratitude to my father for being tough, but FAIR.

Back then, if you'd ask me, "What are your parents?" I'd probably start to literally shake at the thought of how annoying and overbearing they were. But, ask me now. After heartbreaks, headaches, overdraft fees, and barely any groceries—my parents have been the one and only constant hope in the midst of this millennial's chaos. Now, I will gladly exclaim,

"They're superheroes with powers of unconditional love, forgiveness, and compassion." So, when the DJ screams,

"Will the real superheroes please stand UP?" Toni & Shawn will be right there—electric sliding & cupid shuffling to the beat of God's divine drum. Thank you for the sacrifices. For every one of your wants, which was set aside, in an effort to fulfill our needs.

Oftentimes, we do not understand our parents, but our parents understand: losing a door at 13 is more bearable than losing a precious life, they fought so hard to nurture, at the fragile age of 20.

This is an ode, to the parents who lay foundation. However you may do that and with whatever resources are accessible; you show up every day/night for us… and we salute your sacrifices.

06

Being a Target - *Bully Days*

"Why you up so early? School don't start til 8:30"
"Ma, I have to be ready—this a big day."
"Go back to bed before I hurt you."
"Maaaaaaaa, can I wear some of your lip gloss today?"
"Damn, Shakia—YES! Now, back to bed, please!"

In fall 1999, I walk into my kindergarten classroom with a heart full of dreams, abundance of aspirations, and a huge smile upon my face. I am so excited to start school because it gives me the opportunity to interact with other children. This five year old girl loves people more than life itself. I walk through the colossal doors of St. John the Baptist elementary school with hopes of one day becoming an influential person.

But as I walk into classroom K-108, not only do the other kids begin to make fun of my appearance, but staff/parents begin to whisper about me as well—I am overweight and have severe eczema. I am escorted out of my classroom in a haste, because the teachers notice the rough, dry, black spots all over my body and think I have a disease, which could possibly infect my classmates. My mom, now annoyed and frustrated, stomps into the school that afternoon to explain that my eczema is a skin disorder that is not contagious. This day begins a trajectory in my life, where people are constantly judging me based off of my outer appearance, before taking the time to get to know me.

My elementary through junior high school years were my "bully days." These were very low points in my life, because I felt alone and unworthy of love. Junior high school offered an ultimate struggle, due to my juxtaposition between the Hispanic girls with long curly hair and bougie black girls with fresh perms/weaves.

In 8th grade, I had dark skin, weighed 200lbs, and wore a size 18/20; I never had the pleasure of shopping at regular child department stores.

Individuals, who posed as my friends in private, denied me in public and often acted as if they didn't know me in school. My mirror constantly heard, "Fat girls like you don't deserve friends." Shame and fear kept me confined to my books and Barbie dolls because I knew they would never disappoint me; my dolls would never call me guerrilla or pull my hair.

There were hours spent in the bathtub, fiercely scrubbing my coarse skin in hopes my eczema and all the pain that came with it would eventually wash away. My insecurities grew inside of me like a well-taken [care of] plant watered by my own self-harm. My doubt produced an uncontrollable desire in me to be an "overcompensating" friend. Always the one ready to fight or take a hit for others who didn't genuinely care for me. Oftentimes, being forced to suppress my interactive nature because I was deemed annoying or doing too much.

I'm 9 years old and I love Jesus, because he's really cool to me. Surprisingly, I'm the kid who loves going to church. It offers me this rare peace. God's voice and hand over my life has propelled me forward [even] through consistent darkness. At a young age, I saw who God was through many beautiful souls who've crossed my path, but I've also learned that church hurt is real and deserves to be healed.

Sunday school circa 2003.

"Why did Jesus flip over the tables in the temple?" my teacher asks. I eagerly raise my hand to answer, but one of the kids whispers to me,

"Because, he saw Shakia and couldn't believe how fat

she was." I put my hand down and sit in silence for the rest of class. Then, I go into the sanctuary; I find a group of teenage girls and try to show myself friendly,

"Hey, did y'all catch that new B2K joint—it's fire!" They look at me in bewilderment.

"Um, don't you have friends your own age?" [That's the problem. I don't have any friends].

Later, I sit next to my godmother and begin to scratch throughout the entire service. My eczema irritates me so much, I break my skin, bleed immensely, and am left with blood-stuck tights. When service is over, my godmother cannot believe what she sees. Members of the congregation stand about 15ft away from me, as if I have a contagious disease. I arrive home in tears, standing in front of my mother in the kitchen, as she's blankly staring back at me. This is a rare moment, when my mom looks empathetic. She wants to help me, but doesn't know how.

But, God uses the anguish I felt during my developmental years as the drive behind my passion to help and inspire others. As Joseph said, "You intended to harm me, but God intended it for good to accomplish what is now being done, the saving of many lives" (Genesis 50:20). I know what it feels like to be friendless and always alone.

Oftentimes, sitting in a corner wishing someone would come along and appreciate me for who I am. This causes me to put my treasures in the hearts of people, instead of in temporary affirmations, such as calling out the boy with bad acne or picking on the girl who wears a double-digit dress size.

The lack of love I received, motivates me to show love to others, because placing a seed of hope in a broken person's heart can have an everlasting imprint on their future. Whenever I see someone alone, I am the creepy girl who lurks up to the table and sits down. Every time I see someone hurting, the 5 year old girl in me comes alive again and I am reminded of those tears I cried every night. Those tears, filled with so much pain and anger, drive me. They propel me forward.

Many people spend their entire lives in a frenzy, trying to forget their bully days—I don't. I take K-108 with me everywhere I go, because these days, I need a reminder of pain in order to push through the rain.

07

Being Time-[LESS] - *Worth Pt 1*

"One glad morning when this life is over
I'll fly away
When I die – hallelujah by & by
I'll fly away
Oh, when I die – hallelujah by & by
I'll fly away
Fly away to a home in the sky, sitting high – oh
I'll fly away"

5 years old I realized I was different—
From all the other little girls.

I had wide hips,
Coarse hair,
Penguin feet.

I was neither Boricua nor Dominicana;
My glory was not found in my Goldie locks or radiant skin.
Rough dark patches—
Which, stretched from my hands down my arm,
And along the crevices of my thighs.

Kindergarten I realized I was ugly,
And could never be beauty.
1st grade troubled toddler—
2nd grade I knew boys would never like me,

3rd grade my period came—
Only girl in the classroom with breasts—GREAT SAVE!
4th grade - certain touches will never feel the same.
5th grade they said, "Anger management is the key,"

6th grade I'll never fit in—
Not even if the God of geometrics descends from the heavens,
Crafts a box made out of ruby red diamonds,
And strategically plants my feet in it.

7th grade I'll never have friends,
8th grade 13 years younger,
200lbs overweight—
Crashing and breaking any bone structure that could possibly work in my favor.

9th grade I couldn't even keep my spine straight—
Bus stops and train rides became familiar territory.
Bullets in my mouth,
Knees sore from the concrete—
I was baptized into the family,

Of every other insecure Brooklyn girl,
whose opinion didn't matter.
Because, like a plethora of political speeches—
Her words were empty.

10th grade [I] started all over—
Funny, because I never knew who I was in the first place.
11th grade I met her—
Our love was so young and pure.

We tried to win a war [armor free].
No weaponry—
Just distant ideologies and theoretical tendencies.
12th grade—by that time,
My mom was so done with me.

Post heartbreak—
Innocence fled from every exit—
I don't remember what God looks like.
I constantly wrestle through jargon,
In hopes of finding a fresh resemblance of something free.

College.

Freshman year—excitement overcame my body.
Certainly, I'd find something new, something original, something me.
Learning how to pray more–
Complain less.
Number 1 rule: Do not let boys use you.
Number 2: Everyday tell yourself you are beautiful.
And 3: Be free.

This was cute—for a little.
But after two semesters of zero love interests and constant manipulation,
I grew weary.

Sophomore year—was worse.
By then, I was more busy and way passed the freshman 15.
Everything I worked for,
Slaved for,
Cried for–

What did He die for?
For this ugly beast –
To walk through life tip toeing on satin sheets –
Breathing in a combustion of deception and heat?

Questions of love, sex, and Christianity –
I never knew what it felt like to just be.

Junior year—I lost a huge part of me.
So, now I live in fear.
I'm afraid of time–
Even worse—losing a single moment.

At an attempt to control life–
I forget to live.
I forget to breathe.

I remember to love everyone, except myself.

I remember to hurt consistently [while still]
Smiling in the face of adversity.

I remember elementary, high school, Brooklyn streets.
Bus stops and train rides.
I remember everything that makes me, me.

I forget that I will never be whole.
No matter how hard I try to put the broken pieces back together–
I shall never see the face of my soul.

I wish I could forget
Elementary,
High school,
Brooklyn streets.
Bus stops and train rides–

I pray to God every day,
I can make my past go away.
That, I can forget everything, which makes me [me].

That, I can one day be FREE.

That, one day I can just BE.

One day, I can just be WORTHY.

Where were you born?_____

_____
_____
_____
_____

If you could only live with one memory [for the rest of
your life], what would it be?_____

_____
_____
_____
_____
_____
_____
_____
_____

Does that memory occur where you were born? If not,
where does it take place?_____

_____
_____
_____
_____
_____

Is the memory happy or traumatic? Which [emotion]
evokes the most change in you?_____

_____

_____

_____

_____

_____

_____

_____

_____

What did that memory teach you about yourself? Did you
learn it in the moment or later on in life?_____

_____

_____

_____

_____

_____

_____

_____

_____

_____

_____

Free Write: "The only way to the other side is through the fire—not around it." What does this quote mean to you? Just write, don't think.

PART TWO: BEING AGAIN

08

Being Loved

It is September 15, 2011 and it's my best friend, Chantelle's birthday. So, I escort her downtown Brooklyn, to her choir rehearsal. We're in high school, which means: that on a friend's birthday, we buy balloons, a cake, and spend the entire day with them (no matter what's going on). As my Chaney is probably singing her lungs out, I sit in a nearby McDonalds sucking on a caramel frappe, until her rehearsal is over. When the time comes, we meet outside of the colossal doors on Jay St, but as we turn to leave, I hear,

"KIAAAAAAAAA!" I turn around in shock,
"Crystal! Oh my god! How are you?"
"I'm good, you know—what are you doing here?" I shove my best friend,
"My girl Chaney goes here and it's her birthday, so we're kicking it."

By this time, an extremely skinny, yet stunningly-sure-of-herself, masculine looking girl is staring at me. I try to avoid eye contact, but her hazel eyes accidentally lock with mine. Crystal sensing the awkwardness,

"This my homegirl Diana."

Everyone chuckles, except for me. I don't get the joke. Diana and I peace each other, Crystal and me exchange goodbyes, as Chaney and I head towards the A train. Before we get to the corner, Crystal yells out,

"Yo. Kia, wait up." She catches up to us,
"My homegirl thinks you're cute [and she like big girls], can she get your number?" I look at Chaney and then back at Crystal,
"Na, but give her my AIM."
At the time, I was a heterosexual woman, who fell in love with another woman. It was the top of my junior year in high school when I met the girl who would eventually come to be my heartbeat and headache for close to two years straight. Now, if you would have told 13 year old me—a strong Baptist believing, boy fanatic—that I'd be in love with ano-

ther female, I'd probably curse you out. Or have gone on a pretentious tangent about how: "I love everyone, but that gay sh*t just not for me—I love Jesus!"

This stems, from a time in my life, where I equated my relationship with Christ to things like my sexual orientation. I was raised to believe that homosexuality is the greatest sin of them all, and I was spitefully putting nails in Jesus' hands and feet when I was involved with someone of the same sex. My love for another woman has affected my faith, altered my relationships, and caused me to deny love.

Every day I choose to bury a part of my story, my mind is forced to forget; that I was ever loved. For that, [self], I am sorry

"

I neglect a part of who I am and constantly lie to myself, in order to make others feel comfortable. This particular love story is such a huge part of me and basically the backbone of my testimony, but I rarely share it.

Why?

Because, I'm afraid to.

When I sit in intimate circles, I'm forced to be shallow. I do not share how my first genuine love was a woman. I live in fear that people will either look at me strange or worse—ask a plethora of obnoxious questions that are irrelevant to the conversation.

So, when all the girls are talking about the boys that they've loved, or the boyfriends who've broken their hearts—I sit in silence.

"Hey Papi, let me get 2 slices and some zeppole…" turning around to face Diana—

"Hey big head, whatcha want to drink?" Barely looking up from her Sidekick LX,

"I don't care."

As I plop my bottom in the tight booth across from my distracted girlfriend—there's coldness in the air. Finally, breaking the silence, I dig,

"You havin fun talkin to other hoes on the phone I bought?" She sucks her teeth,

"Here you go…you been talking to your friends again, huh?"

Our slices come out of the hot brick oven, but all appetites have left. Instead, this tiny pizzeria is filled with silent minutes and unkind stares from across the table. Finally, I get up to leave—alas, four eyes stare up at me. Quickly, before she can stop me, I interject,

"Na—don't worry about me…make sure whoever gotcha so distracted, worth it." Attempting to break me,

"Why you gotta be so insecure?" Not having it this time—

"And why you gotta be such a b*tch?"

Those 2 years with Diana were far from perfect. She cheated, lied, and manipulated my weaknesses, just like any man would have. The bond was often bent, but never fully broken. Meanwhile, I'll act as if this love affair never even existed; most importantly, I allow societal norms to illegitimate my experience.

I know that I am a woman, who was in love with another woman. The love we embodied was just as powerful and real as if I was a woman in love with another man. She even broke my heart like a man would have, but I don't feel comfortable or safe enough to share that with many people. I even convince myself that my love with *her* will never be as sacred as my love with *him*.

At a time, when people asked me, "Are you still a virgin?" I'd reply with a hesitant "yes," even though I'd encountered almost every sexual experience with a woman. Fearfully, I'd still hold onto this dirty sense of purity, as I allowed society to construct my internal definitions of love, sex, and sacredness. I made myself believe I was still a virgin, because

I'd never been fully intimate with a man—and that's the way it should be, right?

Truthfully, my being is crafted in the image of God and I do not want to disappoint my creater. Am I disappointing God when I fall in love with another human with my same genetic code? I'm asking, because I genuinely do not know the answer. In an effort to move-on, I'd rather forget all the moments spent [entirely].

But, what happens to the bond we built together? The intimacy we created with one another? The love? It begins to not exist. To not be able to share such a vital part of my life story with those I hold close to my heart; just because I've been forced to believe, "It's not the right way of doing things" kills me. I feel a pain that I cannot even describe in words, when I think about the most formative two years of my life and then make myself believe that they never existed. Every day I choose to bury a part of my story, my mind is forced to forget; that I was ever loved. For that, [self], I am sorry.

09

Being Cold - *A Reflection*

Where do you find your peace?
Honestly son...I'm still looking for it...

I watched her die,
I heard her cry,
I saw her scream—
 Who was *she*?

Was she the product of the *dream*?
She was progress.
At least that's what they told me.
But, not really what they showed me.

Her life full of innate sorrows and constructed joys;
Harlem hospital—
College grad—
No dad—
Laid off—
Alcoholic—
Grandmother—
Chain smoker.

I watched her soul wander,
Lips swell,
Skin get pale—
Heart shrink.
Her body got weaker as breaths became fewer.
Inhale scarcity—exhale sanity

I remember, when she couldn't make it to the corner store [no'more].
Instead, her brown eyes pierced through the bottom window;
As she chased concrete pavements with dilated pupils.

Vision blurred—insides stirred
Life span shortened;
Woven together with covert oppression,
Cigarette smoke,
And Bacardi gold.

This was the deterioration of Harlem's *soul*.

She knew no sorrow;
Like being the product of a system that worked.
It succeeded at failing her,
Passing her.
Run faster–

Then, [just] maybe you can catch up to your forefathers' apprentice.
No health insurance–
Hard working woman,
Broke her back on hardwood floors from the age of 15;
And [still] they didn't even find her worthy of sustainable social security.

Guilty pleasures ruled her world.
She was no longer that little girl in Harlem...
Playing double-dutch on those Brooklyn streets
Boogie down Bronx was mean,
Eating Pastrami sandwiches on 150th street.

She was broken.
Laid out–
Put to sleep–
Searching for peace.

And I'm still here – weakkk!

Worrying about the fate of her eternity.
Sitting on hospital floors everyday–
Trying to learn how to pray;
To a God, who has the ability to save her soul.
Sweating out all these tears–
Cold fears chilling the atmosphere.

I LOVE HER!

I want to tell her.
But, now is the final stage–
Her brain is a cloud,
And she doesn't even remember my name.

I wonder if she dreams about me?
Thinks about when she bought me my first bike?
Or stopped them girls from stealing all my fight?

Is she happy?
Or bitter about the face of her future?
Does she know how much I love her?

Her story is for you..
For all the colored girls in this world—
Colored women who feel like their best is NEVER good
enough.

For, those of us—
Who gave it all up.
To a man, who will then white-wash our soul;
Can't even afford to put you in a decent nursing home.

But.. at least you got your card playing,
Bowling alley swinging,
Legion Street drinking,
Apollo singing memories.
I don't need your textbook to know my history –
What it took for me; to get here.
All those blood, sweat, and tears.

It took 250 years of lashes,
99 years of ruthlessness,
Jim Crow—redlining.
It took grandma,
It took Harlem,
I took Brooklyn.

I watched her die,
I heard her cry,
I saw her scream,

Who was *SHE*?

She was *ME*...

In Loving Memory of

Marlene Patricia Wright

10

Being Her - *Grandma's Song*

"What is your biggest regret in life?"
"Being away so frequently during the last years of hers."

It is a sweltering July day in Brooklyn, as I look up at my three-story brownstone in amazement. This isn't the sandy beaches of Hawaii but its home—my home. I turn back to the car, wave goodbye to my mentor, and begin to drag my heavy suitcase up the concrete steps. Now, jaded and out of breath, I run downstairs to see the woman I've missed the most.

I expect her to greet me with a smile, hug, or even a kiss. But, when I open her bedroom door, my grandmother's crawled up in a ball—she has to weigh less than 80lbs—with her hip bone showing through her dry and cracked skin. I keep calling her name, but she doesn't open her eyes. For a few minutes, I stand over her in utter disbelief. Is the smartest and most feisty person I have ever come into contact with gone?

Now hyperventilating, I call my mother, but since she works underground her phone keeps sending me straight to voicemail.

Running back upstairs, to find my father sound asleep in his bed—I shake his a** like an Earthquake,

"How long has grandma been like this and why haven't you guys taken her to the doctor?" He wakes up in a fright, confusedly looks up at me, and says,

"Well, hello to you too. But, some of us work around here and can't make her do anything she don't wanna do!"

Marlene Wright was born August 21, 1938, in Harlem—temporarily confined to The Bronx, but ultimately a Brooklyn girl. She loved to bowl, party, and drink. Crossword puzzles, Sudoku, and unforgettable acts at The Apollo turned

She only expected me to be original and never imitate the lives of others. She'd always say, "Teenages should be their own person ..."

"

her gloomy nights into brighter days. Original number one Dodgers fan every season they played for Brooklyn. Smart as a whip. I mean, she was a walking dictionary—even though she'd never unveil the meaning of a word. Instead, she instructed me to, "Go look it up yourself."

Marlene was a working girl—she worked her entire life, from the age of 15—and never allowed others to diminish her pride. She bought me my first bike, picked me up from school every day, and paid my phone bill every month [right up until the day she died].

There was no judgment between us, which is pretty amazing, since I made a lot of mistakes during my teenage years. She only expected me to be original and never imitate the lives of others. She'd always say, "Teenagers should be their own person and never pick up bad habits." She was my star, but her bad habits stopped her song before I was ready to let go.

I walk back into my grandmother's bedroom. This time her eyes are open, but she's not fully aware of her surroundings. I get her up out of the bed, bathe, and clothe her. She can hardly breathe, as I sit her on the toilet to cut/ style her hair. As soon as my mother drags her feet through the door from a long day of hard work, I insist,

"Ma, I'm calling Aunt Mildred, then we're calling the ambulance, and she's going to the emergency room—no more waiting!"

After that, everything moves so swiftly; my aunt comes to our home—then the ambulance. We spend hours in an emergency room filled with patients who range from criminals with gun-shot wounds to non-English speaking elderly residents with 3rd degree burns—it's Bushwick, what can I say? After about 8 hours of no communication from the hospital staff, a nurse directs me to the doctor on call who explains,

"It seems that your grandmother is experiencing the final stages of her Chronic Obstructive Pulmonary Disease. We can work to try and lessen her symptoms so she can feel as comfortable as possible, but there is nothing we can really do to help her at this point."

This day, begins my heart wrenching journey of having to watch the woman I love most disintegrate before my eyes. One lung disease caused my 74-year-old grandmother to become completely immobile. During that time, she could barely eat or talk due to the breakdown of her respiratory system. Similarly, she became mentally ill because of the lack of oxygen to her brain. The doctors were right—there wasn't much they could do for her.

  She died a month later. I get it—grandmothers die, we all know this. But, when it's your grandmother being put into the ground, it feels different. It feels heavy. I don't know what makes this so hard for me. I've experienced death before. But, this is different—this is BIG. Too big for me to sit with at times. Though my grandmother was sick for a long time, the final stages of her disease came so swiftly and I [still] was not ready.

  Usually, I want to ball up the hurt, make an imaginary baseball bat, and hit a home-run with it. She'll like that, because baseball was her thing.

  How can something come suddenly, yet feel so drawn out? It may even be the logistics of having a sick grandma with no health insurance, benefits, or collateral. Being treated as trash in the system; constantly surrounded by people who want to help her, but can't. My grandmother's presence taught me how to live, but her death still teaches me how to be alive.

11

Being Disorderly - *Fat Girls Do Cry*

"So, can I talk to you real quick?"
"Yea, what's up son?"
"Um, I just, really like you—you know? Like.. more than a friend?"
"Oh, well you're everything I look for in a girl, but you aint pretty enough to claim."

6th grade's going pretty well. I'm on first honors, have yet to be suspended, and actually have a few friends. Today, one of my few friends decides to get in trouble. Meet Paul—the light skin, relatively short, and seldom comedic pre-teen boy that is the "best boyfriend in my head." In reality, Paul and I are actually friends; I just have a crush on him, which means in hindsight we're far from friendly.

Don't worry—this confuses me as much as it confuses you. Anyways, Paul is sitting outside the principal's office, because today he went on a comedic tangent in the wrong classroom. Meanwhile, being a great and thirsty friend, I decide to visit him. As I walk out of history class, bathroom pass in hand—with no intention of going to the bathroom—a life-altering internal decision is made:

Today, I will tell Paul that he is the only guy I've ever loved and express my want to spend the rest of my life with him [which seems particularly valid for a couple of 11 year olds].

I get to the principal's office, swallow hard, and take a dreadful walk to Paul's bench. Everything's going well at first, as we talk about mystery meat Mondays and incomprehensible math homework. Until I aim for the kill,

"Um, I just want to tell you that I really like you." He briefly looks around to ensure that this is actually happening; after too many seconds of silence, he reluctantly responds,

"Oh … what do you mean?" I decide to dig an even bigger hole.

"You know, as more than a friend." And, good-ole Paul buries me in it,

"Ah, cool cool...." As he places his hand on my shoulder,

"Well, you're everything I look for in a girl, but you aint pretty enough to be my girlfriend...sorry but I can't claim you."

After Paul unintentionally broke my heart, I thought about crying, screaming, or even running away (I was a dramatic kid). But, I did none of the above. Instead, I pondered on, "Why is this happening to me?" He wasn't interested in me, which is digestable, but why would he say something so blatantly mean and destructive to me? I concluded, Paul—along with the rest of society—believes "fat girls don't cry."

Meaning, since I am fat, I will have no problem being a permanent member of the friend-zone, am immune to pain, and incapable of hurt. This altercation was merely the first round to a string of events that followed throughout the rest of my life. Mainly, because people infer that fat girls have no sorrows that a 2-piece and biscuit from Popeyes cannot fix.

For me, this was the case; I became an uncontrollable binge eater, because eating fried chicken at 3am was a lot more comforting than thinking about the pain Paul caused me. That was, until I purged all the chicken wings and fries, as I sat in a pool of tears on my bathroom floor. I had the ability to master everything, except my weight. No matter how much I starved, purged, or stretched myself, my weight always won. Regardless of the honors, accolades, or awards I received, my insecurities were always at the forefront.

"Damn, this corset is so tight," I plead as I try to squeeze into my size 14 dress. My roommate walks in,

"You look great girl!" I hear her, but am so distracted by my back-fat, her words go in one ear and out the other.

As I sashay out the door (you know, feel like crap but give off fabulous) I respond,

"Thanks love, see you later."

Moments later, I arrive at lunch with a friend—Konner. Konner is beautiful, thin, and blonde. I love her, but I don't understand how regular human beings can look like celebrities; it's not fair game for the rest of us! Anyways, when it's time to order, all I can think is,

"Why do people always want to go out to eat? I shouldn't eat any of this... but salad sounds like a waste of money." Konner interjects my mental tangent,

"So, what are you going to get?" Before I can respond, she blurts out,

"I think I'll get the loaded calzone with mashed potatoes on the side and extra butter."

I cannot control my eye-roll; before I can answer the waitress [now visible], hovers over us.

"You gals ready?"

"I know what I want," Konner explodes, "You ready?"

"Sure, I'll have the tuna sandwich on wheat with a side salad—and water with lemon please."

We eat, catch up, and have an overall good lunch. The waitress collects our plates and I can't help but feel like a complete failure. I should have only gotten a salad—*why get the bread sis?* After going over options in my head, I finally excuse myself from the table—it is a dreadful walk to the bathroom. I enter the bathroom, turn on the faucet, and begin to purge myself. I wipe my mouth, wash my hands, and reapply my lipstick; I think to myself,

"Hopefully I got all the carbs out."

That wasn't the first or last time, I attempted to get

"all the carbs out." If life was only that simple. Imagine, if one day I can wake up and purge all the carbs, fat, stretch marks, and hurt? Would I be happier? Would my life be in order? Would Paul have liked me? Would I have liked myself?

As my life evolves, the answer for me is no. Altogether, I've lost 60lbs in less than 12 months and still wake up with the same feelings of hurt, shame, and guilt. Will my mind ever stop finding flaws? I don't know. But I do know that I have been given this life, body, brain, and heart. You may ask, "for what reason?" I'm still trying to figure that out. Meanwhile, I will attempt to cherish the gifts and life I've been given. Lastly, I will always feel like a fat girl—with or without a disorder.

I'm here to tell the world that fat girls do cry.

12

Being Fraudulent - *Reality Vs. Reckoning*

"What's your best feature?"
"My mouth."
"Why?"
"It can get me out of any situation?"
"How?"
"I can always use my words to convey a distorted version of
my reality."

My heart bleeds with every loud beat of sorrow...
Someone borrowed my tomorrows
And never gave them back.
So, [for some reason] I'm still stuck in the past.

And I know it's time for me to break free,
But I just don't have the courage to believe.
All those tears I cried on Macdonough St,
You'd think I'm the reason, the grass is green.

Work all week.
But, still-- there's never enough money.
Pretending so much,
It's beginning to penetrate me.

Seep into my skin.
Sunken and placed [deep] within my own misery.
I just had an epiphany, I need to go to *Bible study*?
Na, I rather chase brown boys in these Brooklyn streets.

This ghetto mess makes my heart beat—
Faster with every lie &
Slower with every line of truth—
It excites me.

As I wash blood off my boyfriend's sheets,
All I can think is, You died for me—
Someone watched their baby bleed to death on Calvary.
You washed me clean, yet I still feel so dirty.

Why does my reality seem so contrary to your plan for me?
Why am I walking dead when you already died for me?
I put my salvation on layaway—
Can barely meet the payments each week—
When you already wiped my slate clean.

Constantly!
Searching for you in the hands of my enemy,
When you already live inside of me.
You're beating on my insides—
Tryna make sure my soul DON'T die.

Yet, I'm still here—
Sitting in this wheelchair—
When you already healed me.
Too scared to walk…
It's as if I've lost all of my thoughts.
These memories work overtime to haunt me.

I'm like Jonah before the whale.
Abraham before Isaac,
Ruth before Boaz,
Daniel before the Lion's Den,
Jesus before the cross –
I need you to carry this torch.
I can't learn peacefully,
You're probably gonna to have to beat it out of me!
Job me,
Son me,
Na - that's weak.

I need some fire–
Who got the trees?
I'd rather two step over a trap beat,
Than confess how much I need Thee–

How much I need something greater
Than myself to get me through hell.
All this fake sh*t is making my throat swell.
Questions often left unanswered.
While lies, take a toll on the truth.

I wish I had the final play,
Or enough miscellaneous days to make up,
For all the ways [in which] I've hurt myself.
But, it's hard to heal,
When you can't breathe.

I can't breathe.

Too many knees pinching my destiny.
Meanwhile, we still can't see -
How all this really fake sh*t,
Is still fake -
Regardless, of how real it seems.

13

Being Stuck - *Depression Session*

"How do you feel?"
"Empty."
"Why?"
"I'm missing something?"
"What, exactly?"
"Myself."

It is October of my junior year in college and I have been blessed with a single in my on-campus apartment, which means, no roommates! There are 57 square tiles on my back wall. I know, because I've counted them repeatedly over the past few weeks. My alarm goes off, but my eyes are already open. I've been awake for about an hour. I silence my alarm, pull back the covers, and reposition myself.

Now, sitting [in silence] in an upright position on the edge of my bed. I sulk for a few minutes as I look directly into the mirror across from me. I want to move, but cannot. I want to walk from my bed to the door, but cannot. I continuously tell myself, "Get up, Get up, Get…, Ge…" Instead, I retreat back under my covers. RINGGGG! It's my supervisor. Ignore. This is the 4th time I've missed work in the last 2 weeks. How do I still have a job?

With tears welled up in my eyes, I stare at the back wall and begin to count:

1 yellow tile, 2 yellow tile, 3 yellow tile, 4 yellow t…, 5 yello…, 6 ye…

I close my eyes, a tear falls, and I drift away to a sleepy utopia. No work, no class, no meeting—just me, myself, and my yellow tiles.

It's funny how we can easily pinpoint our previous problems, once we no longer struggle with them anymore. During this time, I didn't know what was wrong with me—I just knew I wasn't myself. I felt stagnant, like a little child stuck in the midst of constant chaos. I was a hopeless soul, just waiting for the hours in the day to go by, so I could spend my next 24 in a comfy bed listening to an array of Neo-Soul's greatest hits.

There were weeks spent, not going to class, work, or into my own living room. My bed was my fortress. Counting tiles and listening to Jazmine Sullivan was my idea of a good ol' time. Also, when I was forced to leave my room, it was very brief and intentional. I went straight to a mandatory class session, avoided personal interactions, and hastily went back to my room.

My mind was telling me, "fight," while my body went into hibernation mode—my limbs wouldn't listen to my mind. This was new to me, because I always had control. Even when I felt broken, I could "fake it till I make it." But, this time, I was all faked out. I gave up, because there was no fight left in me. At the time, I didn't realize I was fighting demons or being weighed down by empty promises and countless apologies (often ones I made to myself). Ultimately, I believed it was just a phase that I'd eventually "get through."

Last semester of senior year has finally arrived. There is so much to be done in so little time. Surprisingly, for once, the pressure does not excite me. Today, I'm finally leaving my yellow tiles—I need a different environment to be productive. Making the difficult decision to troop it to Tara's dorm, I take the long and cold walk from one side of my campus to the other. There's only one thought on my mind,

"I hope Tara still has that bottle."

After fighting with snow and sleet, I finally arrive at Tara's dorm. As she opens the door, we barely make eye-contact, but our hearts feel the depth of the silence. I come inside and run up the stairs behind her. Tara sits on her bed, as I begin to undress the abundance of layers needed to avoid frostbite. Still, no words have been spoken, but my coldness is as strong as this Massachusetts winter. Before I can unpack my bag, Tara's hand is outstretched in front of me—there is a bottle of Hennessy in her possession.

I look up at her with a tear in my eye, as I snatch the bottle from her possession. Swig one… swig two… swig three… ahhhhhhh. Then, I scream out,

"Now, we can get some work done!"

Though, this resembles insanity, Tara merely chuckles in an effort to normalize my alcoholic dysfunction.

It came to a point, where people began looking for me. Friends and loved ones were searching for the Shakia they'd known for years. But, I couldn't point them in the right direction, because I was searching for myself as well. Energetic, fun, and confident [me] went AWOL and I didn't know where to begin the hunt. There was a lingering defeat in my eyes that was easier to hide in the beginning, but as time progressed, it was more difficult to cover up.

I can lie and say, my grandmother's death caused this, but I want to be honest with you all. Standing by, helplessly as a piece of my being dropped into the Earth, broke me, but it didn't cause me to go into an ongoing depression. It triggered a monster that was already inside of me, waiting for it's time to shine. My entire life has been a cover-up. Keeping myself busy, in an effort to cover up my pain. Gossiping about and hurting others as a way to avoid my own feelings of shame.

But, you cannot put a bandage over an open wound and expect it to heal. Sure, for a while, the wound will be covered, but it will eventually become infected and worse off than it initially was. I've learned the hard way, that when I don't properly handle my transgressions, they come back to haunt me in unimaginable ways. Being stuck in my own sorrow taught me that I need to wholeheartedly love, forgive, and cherish myself.

If I don't have the courage to make necessary changes now, the smallest stone can cause my [future] glass house to

SHATTER.

14

Being Brook-[LYIN] - *Worth Pt 2*

"One glad morning when this life is over
I'll fly away
When I die – hallelujah by & by
I'll fly away
Oh, when I die – hallelujah by & by
I'll fly away
Fly away to a home in the sky, sitting high – oh
I'll fly away"

Dear Daughter,

I'm writing you this letter,
Because I want you to learn from my mistakes.
It's time to breathe hope down your throat–
Shake you out your coma.
Cause life is a present and time is too precious.

You think you have an eternity to get it right,
But [truth is] you can't recycle time.
When it's gone, there ain't no get back–
[So] now, all I have are the memories of my past.
Sweet tomorrows, which reflect my sour yesterday's...

Boys – boys
Brooklyn – Brooklyn
Brooklyn boys – boys
Broken boys – boys
My boys – boys.

I watched them fall like leaves,
Off the feeble branches of my apple tree–
Rooted in sin and shaped in iniquity.
If all is well, my degree has elevated me,
And you don't have to worry
About your dreams falling on concrete.
I promise to plant them in rich soil.

[Even] if I have to use tears,
From previous years–
I will water you; nurture you.
You will grow.
I promise to do everything I can,
To ensure unfamiliar voices and cold hands,
Don't sneak into your bed in the darkness of the night
And steal all your fight.

Nor thieves or killers of men
Will be able to invade your precious pearls–[precious]
Precious you are!
Just don't waste a decade
Trying to discover your true beauty–
You are royalty.
Don't be like the 3-year-old version of me,
The little girl I used to be.

She's still somewhere inside these organs–
Playing hopscotch in a barren garden.
Dressed in her Sunday's best–
Searching for purity amongst the dead roses!

She's sinking in a pit of her ex-lover's spit.
I ain't never learned how to swim;
And there sho ain't no lifeguard in the distance.
But, you [my dear] don't have to worry,
About drowning in your own sea of forgetfulness.

DO NOT LET boys use you–
You are not a toy!
You're body isn't Barbie–
It's a Britannica–
Endless pages of our victory
Can be found in the bowels of your belly.
Your bosom has been used to feed men that constructed temples,
Which rest in the center of Egypt.

Matel could never imagine
A goddess, so fitting–
So, this world will throw enough scandals at you;
Now look–
You's a mistress.
In a world that is everything but patient–
Please, learn how to adequately tell time...

Will love be replaced with lust?
Commitment with one night stands?
Or an eternity with temporary kisses?
When eviction notices come 10 days too late;
You realize you're the only resident in this halfway house.
Half-stepping in and out of his bed & His blood.
Trust me, I was young once too –
I know exactly what a broken heart can do.

All those years,
Of God counting my tears..
To turn my back on Him;
For some conditional love,
Who couldn't even stay the night.
Sweat, sex, and seduction lingered on my satin sheets...
Satan was living inside of me,
And I didn't know how to get him out!

Because my soul was tied up
In another brother–
Without a mother.
You do not need another lover;
If you do not know how to love yourself.

Babygirl, don't ever be afraid to ask for help.
When you taint the potter's touch,
With sweaty hands and rubber gloves.
When your sweat glands are filled with the kush of,

Boys – boys
Brooklyn – Brooklyn

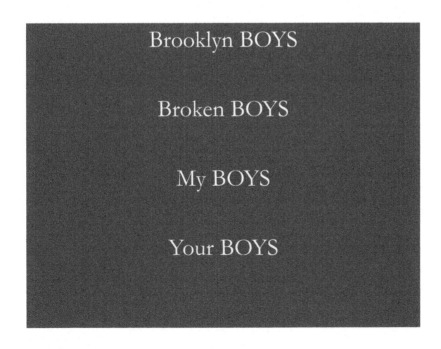

Brooklyn BOYS

Broken BOYS

My BOYS

Your BOYS

NOTES

List three things you've learned [from a person, place, or experience] that you utilize the most in your everyday life?__

_____

_____

_____

_____

_____

List one practice you was forced to unlearn? Why did you choose to let go of something you once held as "truth?"__

_____

_____

_____

_____

_____

_____

_____

_____

_____

_____

_____

_____

_____

_____

_____

Do you learn more from positive or negative experiences?
Why?_____

_____

_____

_____

_____

_____

_____

_____

Free Write: How do you know you're [really] free from so-
mething? Just write, don't think._____

_____

_____

_____

_____

_____

_____

_____

_____

_____

_____

_____

_____

_____

_____

PART THREE

Being Born
AGAIN

15

Being Enough

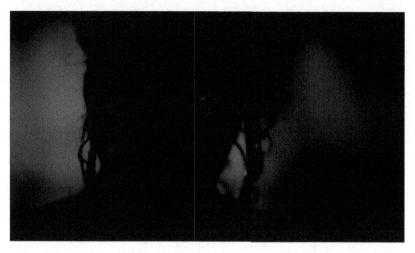

It's the summer after my junior year of college. I'm 20 years old and need to develop better habits. But, what does "better habits" even mean for a dysfunctional millennial like myself? Anyways, as the Brooklyn sun rises, the loud vibration of my phone awakens me. I turn over with crust still in my eyes—it's Latrell:

"Good morning beautiful." Already agitated,
"How can I help you this morning Trell?"
"Is your moms at work?"
"I would think so, but you can call her since you're so concerned about my momma." He gets indignant,
"Can I come through or na?" Finally, the question I've been waiting for.
"No." Now, he's confused.
"What you mean?"
"I said no & it has nothing to do with my momma—I just don't wanna play." As he underestimates my seriousness,
"Come on—stop fronting. I'm about to hop on the train just now." My patience is up.
"No. I'm better than a drive-thru n*gga—make reservations next time."
"What's good with you? Why you stay switching up?"
"Because I'm realizing ain't nothin in my life gonna change - unless I change it."
Before he replies, I silence my phone, roll over, and fall into a peaceful slumber.

Trell calls me the queen of "switching up," which I low-key am, but, have you ever [just] had enough?.

I'm tired of giving people permission to use me. I refuse to place the burden of my own insecurities on Trell or any other person I've allowed to walk off with all my stuff. Though, they've kicked me while down, I won't give them credit for putting me there. There is a difference between one benefiting from your weaknesses and one actually creating inferiority within you. From birth, this world has made me feel inferior, less-than, and inadequate. A.R.E.A.M (Acceptance Rules Everything Around Me).

Due to my longing for acceptance, I'll do anything for temporary love from people who will never stick around after the curtain closes. People will take all my gems, handwork, and respectability—then, when I have nothing left to give and the freak show is over, *where are they?* All the people lined up for my circus act will suddenly disappear.

But *why?*

Not why people do it, but why do I allow them to? Why do I place the knife in the hand of my enemy, so that they can stab with it?

Current conclusion: my life is like Instagram—I do it for the likes. But, I'm tired of doing it for the "likes;" now I want to do it for the love. My life is starting to feel too endangered and an altercation needs to occur. But, where do I start? How do I practice self-assurance in the midst of all my flaws? Will I ever be *enough?*

It is the beginning of my final college semester and I've just come back from a semester abroad in Los Angeles. As the piercing cold hits my flesh, I anxiously walk to the campus student center. There is a mix of excitement, nervousness, and average senioritis going through my veins. Finally, I reach the center and rush into the warmth; various students immediately rush up to me;

"OMG, I've missed you so much–"

"You look so great...No, like you really look amazing."

I fake a smile [have to act cordial or I'll begin to scare the white people] as my head nods. I break away from the crowd, grab lunch, and wait for my friend at a hidden table. As I stick a spoonful of spinach into my mouth, Jack approaches me.

"Oh hey, I've missed you." A little taken aback, I awkwardly get up from my chair to hug him. He greets me with an unusual,
"Oh my, look at you. How's everything been?"
"Everything's been good.." As he grips tighter, he reaffirms,
"I see you're doing good—you look really good."

Serenity, courage, and wisdom will follow me all the days of my life; when they don't, I will offer myself enough grace and space to continue to move forward—even in the midst of my mess.

66

Despite the fact that I've had a crush on Jack since his initial arrival onto my campus, I act unimpressed. Usually, I'd be flattered, but his compliment leaves a bad taste in my mouth; I just nod and smile. He continues,
"We should get together sometime soon." I respond in disbelief,
"Na, we probably shouldn't, but thanks for finally noticing me."

You may be wondering, *why would she turn down a date with a guy she's liked for years?* Because, I'm not a fan of guys who find me invisible, until I'm 40lbs lighter. If I wasn't enough before, what makes me enough now? If every decision I make stems from the narrative, "I am valuable," I will no longer make decisions based in fear. If I am aware of my value and worth, I will make decisions to enhance my life—not deteriorate it.

Meaning, I will embody a healthy lifestyle, as a way to value my body. But, I won't purge and belittle myself, because I cannot fit into a socially constructed ideal. I will submit myself to my life-partner, because of a mutual respect and love we share for one another. But, I will not become dormant and unheard, because I'm afraid of loneliness.

My strength allows me to forgive others and myself. While my humilty, enables me to continuously grow and not stay stagnant.

Current project: work on and mold my senses to feel as if I am enough.

How?

I cannot offer a specific regimen, but I will pray every day, write down my fears, and continue to search for peace to accept all the things I cannot change. Seek therapy and simply ask for help when I need it.

Serenity, courage, and wisdom will follow me all the days of my life; when they don't, I will offer myself enough grace and space to continue to move forward—even in the midst of my mess.

Every day, I will tell myself, "I am enough."

16

Being Flawed - *Who Woke Up Like This?*

"What's the first thing you do when you wake up?"
"Truthfully – check my phone."
"What do you see?"
"An array of beautiful women on Instagram."
"How does that make you feel?"
"Inadequate."
"What do you do with that inadequacy?"
"Thank God for my insecurities and ask that it doesn't hinder my destiny."

It's 6:55am and I beat my alarm by 5 minutes. What shall I do? Instagram! As I scroll through the gram, I see the usual good morning posts, breakfast pictures, and last night's club attire. I double tap on a few photos, until one bold square stops me in my tracks. It is the picture of a vibrant, young, and beautiful woman. She is an up and coming actress, model, and musician; did I mention she's gorgeous. There is a long heartfelt caption,

"Your smile brightens every room you walk into… Your light will be missed… I cannot believe you're gone—RIP."

I continue to scroll and see more pictures [of same woman]—various people paying their respects to the young star and sending condolences to her family. She committed suicide that morning. This talented "X-Factor" winner just finished an overseas tour with her singing group. Shortly after the tour concluded, she was found in her closet, hanging from a clothing rod. She was 25 years old.

Usually, when I check Instagram, I am bombarded by images of women I want to look, dress, and be like–essentially, I want their lives. The oversaturation of small waists mixed with pretty faces/filters, often leaves me in a space of doubt. Will I ever be attractive as my bare self? Even if I see myself as beautiful, will others in this world see me that way?

But in this moment, all I can think is:
"If that gorgeous girl had something I possess, she may still be alive."

How many of us feel like we're missing out on something greater? Honestly, as human beings we are always comparing ourselves to other people. By admiring others, we sometimes shine a negative light onto all the things we lack. I've come to the conclusion that most people, including myself, always want to live life on the other side of the fence.

From infancy, I've often heard, "the grass isn't greener on the other side." Though, my everyday interactions simply disagree. For example, regular people want to be celebrities for all the fame and perks, while celebrities want to be regular, so they can live a private life surrounded by genuine people.

Is the thrill, worth the time, it will take you to rebuild... those things that money cannot buy?

8 7

Mental health awareness is for ALL people. Whether flawed or flawless, please find your light and follow it until your last day.

- Kia Love [loves] you

In the end, our need to always want what other people have can be extremely detrimental to our lives. Our longing for the "finer things" can be very counterproductive, leave us hurt, and often alone. Growing up, I always had the most beautiful friends (by Brooklyn's standards)— light skin, nice hair/weave, mixed breed, big booty, etc. And, I always wished I had their outer-appearance, so I could receive more attention and stop getting friend-zoned. But, I wasn't the teenager who got pregnant, STDs, or had to fear that guys were pretending to love me just so they could have sex with me.

Don't get me wrong, I've [too] experienced my share of heartbreaks and infidelities, but watching my "pretty" friends get dragged through the mud, gave me another level of respect for their pain and suffering. The same way society thinks, "fat girls don't cry," we often believe "pretty people are emotionless," which is the furthest thing from the truth.

8 8

"You ready to be out or what," I hear as I put the final touches on my makeup. I peer out the window to remind my best friend;

"H*e, you needa wait a minute and lower your voice—my mom's asleep." I rush through my eyeliner, check on my mom's slumber, and tip-toe out the door. Before I can fully turn the lock, my best friend whispers,

"It's about time—you got the money?" I turn around with a sigh, take out the money I stole from my mother's wallet, and hand it to her—

"Yo, this all I could get."

"Oh, this good—we should be able to get a bottle and a nick."

"We? I know you ain't talking about me, so who else coming?" My best friend showcases her irritation;

"Why you gotta be like that? You need to grow up and stop acting like a little girl—would I let anything happen to you?" Now afraid,

"I don't know, but I'm really not trying to be out here with these smuts tonight." She responds,

"Well, you can go back in the house or come with me—the choice is yours."

I choose to follow her lead. Later, we arrive at an empty trap house with about 7 young boys. After awhile, everyone is high except for me—[no bad habits yet]. The night strings along dreadfully and my best friend can't fulfill her promise. Things happen that I don't want to happen. As I lay bare on a rotten cot, tears flow from my eyes and all I can think is, *"Why am I here?"*

I had temporary fun in high school lying to my mom, running after boys, and acting crazy. But, when the boys broke my heart and all my friends left me high and dry, I quickly realized [then], that my mom was the only true warrior in my corner. It's funny how most tables always find a way to turn; I'm just grateful I didn't burn every bridge I needed to [later] cross.

I stepped on the heart of my hero, because I valued mundane and lifeless love from my peers. People, who honestly never had the capacity to really care for me. This is the same thing I did to my relationship with Christ. I threw Him away because I valued the treasures of this world more than our relationship. I didn't want to wait on God's timing, because I wanted instant gratification. But, it was like trying to cook filet mignon in a microwave. My life is so much more valuable than an expensive piece of steak, yet I treated it like a pre-made burger from White Castle. Why can't I see the worth in myself, when the creator of the universe lives inside of me?

Sooner than later, that Brooklyn roller coaster came crashing down and the thrill wasn't fun when I was plummeting into the ground at the speed of light. This taught me to cherish everything I have—even those things I deem as flaws. The [very] things that I am complaining about, someone else is praying for! God has carried me through many bad decisions for a reason!

Will you join me in trying to appreciate every new day? Not just saying it, but actually doing it:

Breathe slower, love deeper, and practice consistency!

Are you willing to throw away your blessings because you're craving another person's lifestyle? Ask yourself: is the thrill, worth the time, it will take you to rebuild? To reconstruct parts of yourself that money cannot buy?

At the end of the day, Beyoncé said it best, "You woke up like this," so live in that moment, regardless of what you think you're missing.

17

Being Free - (A)s (F)requently (A)s (P)ossible

"Define freedom."
"The act of being free."
"What is being free...?"
"Being a crackhead, in a crackhouse, choosing NOT to
smoke crack."

"Happy birthday big head," my mom yells to me.
That's right—it's my birthday and I'm finally 20. As I roll
out of bed, my phone vibrates—let the plethora of text mes-
sages roll in; I love all the attention that birthdays brings. It's
from my ex-girlfriend.

"Happy birthday missy—live it up!"
"Haha–thanks," is the only reply I can think of.

Then, I begin to Facebook/Instagram/Twitter stalk
her. [What? Haven't spoken to her in awhile.] As I scro-
ll through, everything seems fine and pretty basic. Until,
a warm Facebook post stops me; it's a picture of a brown
lady's ring finger. Yes, there's an engagement ring on it. The
caption reads,

"I finally asked my queen to marry me."

An instant wave of, "What the f*ck," comes over me.
I don't want to marry her, but after two and a half years was-
ted, don't I reserve the right to be emotional? [Let me answer
this for you]... Yes, TF I do. But, surprisingly, I'm not.
All I can think is, *"I'm about to watch someone I love, com-
mit her life to someone else and I could care less."*
My mind is telling me to be angry, sad, and crazed,

while my heart is content and secure. For the first time, in a long time, I feel free.

This past birthday, as I thanked God for another year, I told myself that I wanted to live slower and love deeper. Now, that sounds quite simple, but it is actually something I struggle with daily. It is so easy to say empty affirmations [repeatedly] to myself, but harder for me to actually act on it.

I can say, "I forgive you; I've let it go" but, is the hurt still in my heart? Well, yes the pain is still in my heart and probably will linger [there] forever. But, I've made a conscious decision to move forward. So, why do I stay stagnant? It's weird because I can be so happy and vibrant for weeks, even months at a time, and then BOOM—rain down random breakdown.

Loneliness creeps up on me like a thief in the night, but the difference is: now, I know how to handle it. How do I channel that pain in productive ways? The answer is simple, "I don't." I do not have the power within myself to show compassion and grace to someone that has shattered my heart.

But, I believe in a God, who gave His only begotten Son, so I wouldn't have to deal with these things on my own. He made it possible for me to go to Him and cast all my worries upon him. He will give me peace.

So, for all the broken hearts and crushed souls: it is not over and you do not have to choose to be bitter. I know, sometimes it feels like an inevitable choice. How can you not be bitter after all the things you've been through? I am not 100% where I want to be, but I can truly say that God gives peace!

Even in the little things like when I watched someone I love, love someone else and was content with that reality. Does my ex deserve loneliness, just because she isn't in a relationship with me? Will I use the little bit of energy left over from my working class day to despise her happiness?

Every time I go to God with hate, I go to him with closed hands. He cannot bless me if I close myself off to Him. I cannot allow others to spew venom into my heart; I am amazing, priceless, and most importantly WORTH IT!

You too, are worthy of love–unconditional and eternal. Allow yourself to experience love by forgiving those who've hurt you; even those who did something you deem to be unforgivable. Don't worry, you don't have to do it alone. You can't do it alone; God has your back every step of the way and when you slip up I promise He will be there to catch your fall. A good friend of mine asked me,

"How do you know you're really free from something?"
My answer: "You don't."

At the end of the day, we think that if we are free or delivered from something, it will just go away. Don't get me wrong, there are instances where that is the case, but not always. Many times, freedom is a daily choice.

Do not be discouraged, because those same feelings or pains creep up in you again—this is normal. Cast it down, pray against those feelings, and work through that situation. Trust the process and don't give up on yourself because you want to go back to destructive ways. Just keep moving forward. Do not think that all of your progress is invalid because you fall short or may still struggle with something.

I struggle with my weight, self-image, and ability to love myself; this doesn't mean that I am the same scared insecure little girl I was in junior high school. Truthfully, I've struggled with these things from childhood and will probably struggle with them for the rest of my life. That doesn't mean I am not an evolving human being. It doesn't mean that I am not constantly growing and becoming who God wants me to be.

However, it does mean that I am making a conscious decision to walk in my destiny. Through the hurt, pain, and doubts, I still know there is a plan for my life, greater than what the eye can see. Ultimately, it means that I am choosing to be free (as frequently as possible).

18

Being ONE - *Bones*

"He led me all around them. I saw that there were very
many bones at the bottom of the valley, and they were very
dry." Ezekiel 37:2

<u>Dry</u> – bare or lacking adornment.

<u>Bone</u> – pieces of hard, whitish tissue making up the
skeleton in humans and other vertebrates.

So, what does that make me?
A bare piece of hard,
Whitish tissue that makes up one body.
This body–
The sacred body that died on a rugged cross on Calvary.

He hung there with nails in both–
His hands and feet–for me.
For this broken vessel.
A church that has the task of loving everyone and everything
wholeheartedly.

To respond to a corrupt world with wisdom and integrity.
Born to stand on solid ground without defeat.
Sworn into the sacred society of victory.

But, what happens when we're standing on the burned souls
of the indigenous people?
Crying babies in Nepal?
Trayvons, Mike Browns, and Baltimore streets.
Where do we retreat,
When life has given us nothing,
But endless amounts of inequities?

Can't even sit in your own home at peace–
Just ask Breonna *smacks teeth*

Then he asked me, "Son of man, can these bones live?" I answered, "Only you know, Almighty LORD." Ezekiel 37:3

I'd like to take you on a journey with me–
It starts on the first day of first grade;
I wanted to move forward...
Instead, I received backlash for being too fat
And an abundance of inedible snacks.

But, there was one girl in the halls of SJB who comforted me–
Her name was Elena;
She came up to me at snack time–
Offered me her milk, I declined, because I'm allergic you see.

So, Elena, must have told her mama about our dilemma.
Because, on the 2nd day of the first grade,
She came back up to me.
I sat there during snack time, with closed palms–
Awaiting in a dark room–

She bounced over to my rescue
And handed me a cartoon of apple juice.
There I was, the only child with a red carton, instead of a white one.
That day, she went out of her way to love me.
At 6 years old, I saw God's soul through her bones.

Then he said to me, "Prophesy to these bones. Tell them, 'Dry bones, listen to the word of the LORD." Ezekiel 37:4

See, justice doesn't always equate to equality.
Loving each other–
Oftentimes, means meeting each other's immediate needs.
Putting down one's self for the sake of another's eternity.
It means loving me enough to help me,
Pray for me–give me the resources I need;

To believe in a God,
Who had every right to stay on the throne of royalty.
But, [instead] descended here to slum it up with me.
Meanwhile, I'm too busy planning focus weeks,
To be the ears to my brother who cannot hear–
Or the hands who wipe the tears from my sister's frazzled
face.

He was pierced in His side,
So I wouldn't have to deconstruct my personality,
To please a majority.
Unification does not equate to assimilation or appropriation.
I need to know when I can't see,
You will be the hands that guide me.

*"This is what the Almighty LORD says to these bones: I will
cause breath to enter you, and you will live." Ezekiel 37:5*

Ezekial told those dry bones to breathe.
And life was created almost instantly.
God has given us the ability to live–abundantly.
He's waiting on us.
To realize our potential–
This race to salvation is expediential;
We can no longer wait until the final days,
To commit to this body.
To do our part, in restoring the longevity,
Of the interconnectivity of 200 and something pieces of
hard, whitish, tissue.

He needs us to do our part in raising these dry bones–
Out of a frozen field of locust–
Packed with depression, anxiety, and national security.

We have the power
–TOGETHER–
To march towards a greater future.
When God says "GREATER,"
He's talking about,
His ability to bring life to a dead situation.

If that doesn't make your femur,
Which is connected to your patella–
Send a spirit of victory to your tibia,
Which is connected to your Fibula–
That will then–
Extend down to your feet and cause your toes,
To give God the glory,
You may not have enough testimony in your body.

*"I will put ligaments on you, place muscles on you, and cover
you with skin. I will put breath in you, and you will live. Then
you will know that I am the LORD."*
Ezekial 37:6

If God can awaken dry bones, imagine what He can do with
the life inside of you.

19

Being Voiceless - *The Underdogs*

"Why do you want to be successful?"
"So, I can show the little homies under me, that it's possible – ya know?"
"What's possible?"
"Being something greater than what you've seen your entire life."

It's the summer after sophomore year of high school and I'm chilling in the park with my boyfriend and his crew. It's June and school has literally just ended; we're still young, free, and naive to the realness of this world. Well, all of us, except Dee—he's brilliant. As I devour my cherry slushy, he begins to teach me about Newton's law. I mean, what else could a couple of high school students in Brooklyn talk about on a hot summer day? Suddenly, his face lights up, as he pulls out his report card and shoves it in my grill,

"See, I go hard—I'ma smart boy son." I challenge,
"But, these are Bs & Cs...you smart enough to get all A's boy?" He directs my attention to his attendance, there are 50 absences for the quarter.
"Dee, why you not going to school son—are you good?" The light leaves his eyes.
"You know, I gotta do what I gotta do—out here in these streets." I'm too young to know how to adequately empathize.
"I know your mom's ain't down with you choosing these streets over your education…"
"Man listen, my moms be more excited to get that money for the cable bill, than to see a good report card from me."

My boyfriend and his friends laugh, while I'm left stuck on stupid.

I'll never forget Dee, because he was my first glimpse into the life of a dream deferred. He showed me that it takes more than talent, motivation, and self-confidence to succeed. Success [also] requires resources, family, love, and hope. Our victory will only be birthed from a faith, ("the substance of things hoped for and evidence of things not seen" Hebrews 11:1), so deliberate that no devil in hell, school system, or prison pipeline can dim it's light. At the time, I was unaware of my own faith. Most importantly, [unaware] of the foundation of all the goodness, which seeped out of me.

After Dee's and I conversation, I realized my hope was built on the love of my family. Especially, on the strength of my parents. My mother wouldn't sell my innocence for a cable bill or crack pipe. Similarly, my father valued me enough to keep his bad habits distant from my present reality. I had role models—good and bad, who gave me options to choose from. Whether my mentor Gabby or third grade teacher, Mrs. Forbes—high standards were always set for me by others who genuinely cared for my being.

Now, I hope to offer myself to others as a resource and imperfect vessel. But, what can I offer someone who thinks they have everything; when [in reality] they have nothing of real substance?

Till this day, Dee is one of the sharpest brothers on the street. Even though, he's still selling his soul for a plethora of name brand clothes and street credentials. What can I give Dee? I can give him my voice, love, and, most importantly, my story.

Harlem
BY LANGSTON HUGHES

What happens to a dream deferred?

Does it dry up
like a raisin in the sun?
Or fester like a sore—
And then run?
Does it stink like rotten meat?
Or crust and sugar over—
like a syrupy sweet?

Maybe it just sags
like a heavy load.

Or does it explode?

I read Harlem by Langston Hughes when I was 13 and even though, I didn't fully understand it, I felt it. Unaware that the feeling his words gave me were due to my everyday interactions with "raisins in the sun." Unaware of the fact that I, too, have always been the underdog.

Where I'm from, most young adults are shown how to apply for Welfare or the Department of Sanitation test before we're even told about college. Not that there's anything wrong with wanting to secure a successful and benefit-packed future for our youth. But, what do we imply about our children's future, when we teach them how to apply for food stamps, but not for scholarships?

How will I view the institution of marriage, if my life is void of committed/monogamous relationships? Will I [still] acquire a strong faith, when I don't have symbols of steadfast individuals? As I begin to grow older, I constantly think,

"How am I going to make people in this world feel something?"

What do individuals need [today], even more than my

money? Is it my physical presence? Is [real] change found in actual time invested? Yes, it is important for me to challenge systems of oppression daily, but I also need to be present with people.

Sitting in a controlled classroom or on a diverse committee, will not stop a young girl in Brownsville from thinking that she is only capable of being a basketball wife or reality tv star. The liberal CNN panelists cannot debate our oppression away. Please, understand that all of these aspects of the revolution are necessary for growth. But, how can I help young brown bodies manifest their "being?" What has the power to affect their mindset?

My opinion: Physically seeing other successful role models who look like and are accessible to them.

People need to see me and feel my refreshing spirit in the midst of their hopelessness. I need to show my young people, an underdog can be victorious.

20 Being Activated - *My Brother's Keeper*

Kendrick Johnson
Raymond Allen
Dante Price
Mike Brown
Breonna Taylor
Glen Patterson

My brothers.
My beautiful brown brothers.
Black brothers.

Jay Z's black album,
Started a blackout in Marcy Projects.
We got the Barclays Center,
But still don't have books.

WEB Dubois would be shook,
If he saw the status of our freedom.
March on Washington –
Keep turning the wheel –
But still no progress.

When the sun goes down,
The freaks come out–
Forgotten ones appear.
Like street lights in the dark night.

AK's, gloc's, and 22's–
My brothers grab their piece–
The only peace they know.
With hearts as hard as stone and blood as cold as snow.

Sandra Bland
Trayvon Martin
Tamir Rice
Maurice Howard
Melvin Lawborn
Daniel Prude

But, even in the midst of all your fallenness–
You're still mine.
I found you.
A raisin in the sun.
Swooped you up and carried you in my bosom.
Back and forth on shattered glass–

Hoping that my tender, love, and care
Could reverse the drought,
You had been experiencing for years.
[That] somehow my tears could water your vacant garden,
And roses may magically appear.

I waited there–
Sat in a sinking pit praying for your soul.
While cold kisses danced on my heart.
Heart attacks from police brutality–
About 50 agents break down your front door
And ramble through your drawers.
In hopes of finding a thief or killer;
But never expecting a scared little boy.

Who wants to be a lawyer.
An artist,
An astronaut,
Or a doctor.

After watching his mom die from breast cancer,
Because she couldn't afford life–
I mean the price of insurance was too high.
He wants to be a doctor –
Now, he wants to save lives.
But you Mr. Officer don't see that when you look into his
brown eyes.

Crystal McDuffie
Michael Wright
Kimani Gray
Tim Stansbury
Eric Garner
Denzell Oglesby

My brothers.
I know we always sympathize with
The mother of the murdered.
But, I'm the sister of the alleged murderer.
My precious blood turned blue when I lost you.
Hopelessness came down like acid rain
On our broken brownstone–

Bed-Stuy opened up and swallowed my home–
The only help I've ever known was gone.
My brother.
You kept me strong;
How can I keep you warm?

Sometimes, I wish you would have spit bars...
Instead, of being confined
By the silver lining of a dream deferred.
What was supposed to happen?
The formula for success,
Was never pissy elevators and dark hallways.

Shawn Wright
George Floyd
Ahmad Arbery
Philando Castile
Robert Fuller
Isaac Arzu

Demons waged war on your soul and I felt it.
I wasn't there,
But I remember when you didn't come back.
When they took you from me,
I saw a boy go from wanting to save lives,
To a man taking one.

My brother.
Even though, you've been led astray
By bullet holes and brown drank.
And shall never [again] see the light of day.
I'm still here,
Waiting to count all your tears.

Because, even my Jesus,
Found room in His kingdom,
For the worst of the worst sinners.

21

Being Historic-[ALLY] - *Worth Pt 3*

"One glad morning when this life is over
I'll fly away
When I die – hallelujah by & by
I'll fly away
Oh, when I die – hallelujah by & by
I'll fly away
Fly away to a home in the sky, sitting high – oh
I'll fly away"

I woke up yesterday,
And things just weren't the same.
Who put that chair there?
How'd this table get over here by these stairs?
Could something so close feel this far away?
There was something …

It was like that fruit in the garden,
Which separated me from you,
Before I was born my destiny was through!
But, it was something...
About that hymn great-grandma used to sing.
I could hear her fight the dead floors,

As her feet bled.
From tears shed,
After watching her son lifeless–
Breathless.
All because Jim Crow said it was his time to go.
I could hear her soul sing chords of hope;
I know I've been changed – the angels in heaven done called
my name.

It was like precious pearls by the sea shore.
Oh God, it was something...
That's when I knew faith the size of a mustard seed;
Could move mountains.
Mount up over the oppression and hurt.
Bullets on the curve,
Click–clack–capow, man down!

You didn't know he was my brother,
You don't care that she's my sister.
Does the prayers of the righteous still have the power to
prevail?
If so, this sweat falling down my face,
Will make a salty lake of strength–
That will not cause me to sink but FLOAT!

The last time I fell to my knees at the altar,
I said to myself–
See, Shakia I know we've been here before but,
I promise this time will be different.
As I clasped my dreary head in the palm of my hands,
I felt God and he whispered softly in my ear.

See, I couldn't hear him quite clear–
Probably because he was drowned out,
By all the Lil Weezy's and Young Breezy's.
Yea, I know I was supposed to give it up–
That drank in my cup...
Along with [those] empty fantasies...
Of one day finding the Hov to my Bey.

Too bad: I never had the courage to believe
In an unpackaged dream.
Before I got up off my knees,
He told me–
Watch the company you keep.
Stay on the lookout for wolves dressed like sheep.

Stubborn and foolish,
I didn't see the need to take heed.

Instead, [I] intentionally made the same mistake twice.
Willingly, gave myself to the world;
Pure and ignorant,
As the fearless girl playing with fire.
So delicately distracted by the burning sensation.

Her ignornace leaves her with no intention,
Of later that day,
Watching the house which birthed her up in flames.
And when they gave me back charred lungs—
Filled with smoke and charcoal,
To replace a once warm beating heart;
 I couldn't dare go back to that same altar in my father's hou-
se.

What kind of bride would I be to a perfect and flawless king?
How could I destroy great-grandma's dream?
Please, send my apologies to Dr. King;
I didn't mean to throw away everything he fought for,
For 30 pieces of silver.
Are gold chains and a mouth full of bling really worth my
soul?

But, see somewhere between my shame and pity party—
Jesus crept into my room in the middle of the night.
I knew it was him, because an array of darkness
Could never overtake his luminous bright light.
He held me.
He wept as I wept.
And hurt like I hurt.
When they shot a fierce pain in my side,
He felt what I felt.

He showed me His hands—
And said stop doubting and believe.
For you have seen.
You didn't destroy the dream.
[You] just took a few detours,
Along your path to the final destination.

The same power that carried great-grandma over troubled water—
Will be the same force,
That lifts you up over barb-wired caskets drenched in molasses.

And, I can hear great-grandma singing...

I know I've been changed – the angels in heaven done called my name

The same blood that worked for her—will be the same blood that works for me.

Which will be the same blood that

works for you.

NOTES

Please look back at your memory from section one. Does it
help you process AFAP (Chapter 17)?_____

_____

_____

_____

_____

Write three things you taught someone this week (either
through words or action)?_____

_____

_____

_____

_____

_____

_____

_____

_____

_____

_____

_____

_____

List 2 Activated practices you can realistically incorporate into your week (Chapter 20)?_____

_____

_____

_____

_____

_____

Free Write: "Being confident in this, that he who began a good work in you will carry it on to completion until the day of Christ Jesus. (Philippians 1:6 NIV) Where do you find your confidence? Just write, don't think._____

_____

_____

_____

_____

_____

_____

_____

_____

_____

_____

_____

_____

_____

_____

ACKNOWLEDGEMENTS

Firstly, it is imperative for me to give honor to God who has graciously extended the love of Jesus Christ and guidance of the Holy Spirit upon me. My being would have stopped a long time ago if not for the hand of God over my life, so I pray these words can be pleasing unto His sight. Though, my words are wrapped with pain, they are [also] birthed in redemption; please know God has the power to heal your being from the inside-out.

To all the warriors who have nurtured and cared for me throughout my life, I thank you. My parents—Toni and Shawn Artson along with my 3 older brothers [Shawn, Michael, & Glen], loving grandmother Paulette Hair, and remaining relatives [near and far]—this compilation of short stories and poems would not exist without you. Especially to the ones who have gone on to the afterlife; I think of you often and pray you live on through me. My hope is that each of you know how greatly you have impacted my life; our family has birthed a new age of being through perseverance and love. Thank you for loving me in the midst of my mess.

To the men and women who have raised me, no amount of words can describe the impact you've had on my being. As a girl, my naivety caused me to doubt many of you, but [now] as a woman, I would not be able to survive without your firm hand and wise teachings.

This is for all the church mothers and street OGs; your impactful stories will live in my heart forever. Thank you to my godmother Ms. Debbie, Aunt Mildred, Mrs. Forbes, Paulea Mooney-McCoy, mentor: Gabby, Ms. Madeline, Sis. Sharon Kelly and countless other contributors to my being. You all have stuck by me through the fire and your love for me has not gone unnoticed.

Similarly to all the teachers, mentors, and advisors placed throughout my life—I appreciate you for seeing light in me when all I saw in myself was darkness. From St John the Baptist grade school to Catherine McAuley Highschool and beyond, angels have consistently been placed in my path through [both] educational and spiritual channels.

While growing up in Brooklyn, faith [unknowingly] was the backbone to my victory. This faith would not exist without the dedication and love from my various church families. To the NYC Baptist community who raised me—I must say thank you for instilling fruits of the spirit within me.

To all the professors who nurtured my hunger for knowledge—your insight and compassion made me never want to stop learning. The Sociology department enhanced my mindset and helped anchor my being. To my amazing advisor: Rini Cobbey and the entire Communication Arts staff: you all literally took lemons and crafted delicious lemonade. I have been able to execute my debut self-publication [independently] because of you all—thank you.

To all of my beautiful friends—who are too many to name, thank you. For checking in, pushing, and loving me in spite of. I pray the telling of our stories, can adequately display my appreciation for our various friendships. Because, you all have allowed yourselves to be vessels of God's unconditional love, the constant turmoil in my life has not been able to take my joy. You all have listened to my ambitious ideas and always encouraged me to shoot for the stars—thank you for believing in, cashapping, and comforting me.

To all the former friends who I've lost, I pray that these stories remind you that our memories are filled with more purpose than pain. If I've hurt you, I pray you can see my heart and choose forgiveness. If you've hurt me, [know that] forgiveness has already been extended from my heart to yours.

To the ones who have intentionally tried to break me, thank you for the most interesting stories I can ever tell. If not for the pain, the manifestation of this book would have never came into fruition. Being abandoned by the ones I held closest [to me], encouraged me to let go of fear and step out on faith!

I express huge gratitude to all the black writers before me. I would not have the courage to tell my story without the unfiltered power that is "black literature." To all my peers in the field who are constantly breaking down barriers for us, thank you for your perserverence and boldness. *Being* would not exist, if your writings did not live [first].

Lastly, to all the brave souls who took a chance on this crazy creative—I appreciate you. For anyone who has contributed to this project in any way, please know you have helped make my dreams come true. John Bucher, thank you for being a consistent advisor, mentor, and friend in this industry. My dear friend and former highschool classmate: Ronide Comeau; your foreward will forever be placed in the center of my heart—thank you for seeing the light in me.
To all the editors, engineers, and producers—thank you for bringing your talents to *Being*. Tanashia Durant, thank you my beautiful Pisces sister for always doing exactly what you say you will do. This project would not be of such high-caliber if not for your advisement and help—I appreciate you sis. My beautiful stylist Stephanie has made me feel more beautiful than I could have ever imagine; appreciate you for working with me and being flexible throughout this entire process.

Huge shoutouts to The Masterz LLC for executing such beautiful images/videos. Iris Designs for producing a phenomenal cover and exemplary brand ID services. The Bowker Agency along with IngramSpark made my first self-publishing experience easy to navigate and extremely affordable. This entire book was designed by me using the Adobe InDesign application—thank you to all the phenomenal digital tutorial creators!

To all of you beautiful souls who found it not robbery to invest in my dreams and buy this book—thank you!

To all the brown girls in city streets: Be yourself. Be whoever you have been birthed to be. Remain consistent, firm in your beliefs, and practice humility. Remember, when the world doesn't see you, I do. Most importantly, God does.

Shakia Love

Born and raised in the Bedford Stuyvesant area of Brooklyn, NY, Shakia dedicates her life to telling unheard stories. Her educational background (BA in Communication Arts & Sociology) coupled with time spent abroad (Central America) has informed her worldview. Years working on-the-ground in urban communities (Girls Inc, Teen Challenge, 808 Urban) fuels her passion for equal representation of BIPOC in digital media.

Her writing style is informed by renaissance artists, such as Langston Hughes and great black authors/sociologists like Delores Williams and Toni Morrison. She finds comfort in modern writers of urban stories and draws inspiration from fellow leaders in the field. She aspires to be as raw and relevant as authors such as, Jasmine Mans and Candice Carty-Williams.

Currently, she lives in Los Angeles where she operates her own Digital Media Agency/Book Publication company. Kickin it Productions LLC promotes the telling of well-rounded stories through education, acceptance, and grace. Through her debut literary work, "Being," Artson hopes to offer the world a humble roar into a new era of story-telling.

Made in the USA
Las Vegas, NV
25 June 2021

25417000R00066